Waste Not
Time to Recycle

by Rebecca Weber

Content and Reading Adviser: Mary Beth Fletcher, Ed.D.
Educational Consultant/Reading Specialist
The Carroll School, Lincoln, Massachusetts

COMPASS POINT BOOKS

Minneapolis, Minnesota

Compass Point Books
3722 West 50th Street, #115
Minneapolis, MN 55410

Visit Compass Point Books on the Internet at *www.compasspointbooks.com*
or e-mail your request to *custserv@compasspointbooks.com*

Photographs ©: Comstock, Inc., cover; Visuals Unlimited/John Sohlden, 4; Visuals Unlimited/Jeff Greenberg, 5, 9, 12; Visuals Unlimited/Bernd Wittich, 7; Visuals Unlimited/Inga Spence, 8, 13, 16; Visuals Unlimited/Peter Holden, 11; Visuals Unlimited/John D. Cunningham, 15; Visuals Unlimited/Wally Eberhart, 17; Visuals Unlimited/Mundy Hackett, 18; Two Coyotes Studio/Mary Foley, 19, 20, 21.

Project Manager: Rebecca Weber McEwen
Editor: Heidi Schoof
Photo Selectors: Rebecca Weber McEwen and Heidi Schoof
Designers: Les Tranby and Jaime Martens

Library of Congress Cataloging-in-Publication Data

Weber, Rebecca.
  Waste not: time to recycle / by Rebecca Weber.
    p. cm. — (Spyglass books)
Includes bibliographical references and index.
  ISBN 0-7565-0387-6 (hardcover)
  1. Recycling (Waste, etc.)—Juvenile literature. I. Title.
II. Series.
  TD794.5 .W383 2002
  363.72'82—dc21
                        2002002757

Contents

Over and Over

Don't throw that trash away!
Did you know that paper,
cans, and bottles can be
recycled? When people
recycle, they find a way
to use something again.

Did You Know?

For every *ton* of paper that people recycle, they save 17 trees from being cut down to make new paper.

5

Find It

If you want to recycle, look around your house or school. Newspaper and computer paper can be recycled. Cardboard boxes can be recycled, too.

Did You Know?

Recycling can mean using something two times instead of one. Recycle your drawing paper by using both sides.

You can recycle many other things. Glass bottles can be melted down and made into new glass. Cans and plastic can be recycled, too.

Did You Know?

The *average* American makes more than four pounds of garbage a day.

ALUMINUM ONLY

Save It

When people find something to recycle, they need to clean it out. Then some cities send trucks around to take these items to a recycling *plant.*

Did You Know?

Plastic bags, candy wrappers, and other trash may end up in rivers and oceans. Animals may think it is food and choke to death on it.

Make It Again

At a recycling plant, big machines crush up old paper to make new paper. Metal cans are melted and made into new cans. This saves trees and keeps people from having to dig up new metal.

Did You Know?
Many places recycle the metal that is in lawn chairs, window frames, and pots and pans.

13

Use It

When you are in the grocery store, look around. Many of the boxes that hold food are made from recycled paper. The cans that hold soda and vegetables are made from recycled metal.

Did You Know?
Recycling one glass jar saves enough *energy* to run a lightbulb for four hours!

14

15

Recycling Outside

Leaves, grass, and kitchen
scraps can be recycled, too.
They can be made into
compost, which is very good
for gardens. It makes the
soil *rich* and helps plants
to grow.

Did You Know?

Each year, Americans throw away more than 24 million tons of leaves and grass clippings.

Save, Save, Save

There are five reasons why people should try to recycle. It saves **natural resources.** It saves energy. It saves clean air and water. It saves **landfill** space. It saves money!

Did You Know?
It takes much less
energy to recycle
paper than to
make new paper
out of trees.

19

Make Recycled Paper

You will need:

- scraps of colorful paper
- water
- a blender
- a piece of metal screen
- a flat pan

Tear the paper into small pieces.

Put five handfuls of paper and two cups of water in the blender.
Blend one minute.

Set the screen over the pan. Pour the mixture onto the screen.

Spread it into a flat layer.

Lift the screen.

The next day, peel your new paper off the screen!

Set it on a towel to dry.

Glossary

average–normal or ordinary

compost–dead plants that are decaying, or breaking down into small pieces

energy–power that can be used

landfill–a place where people's garbage goes

natural resources–things in nature that people use, such as coal and trees

plant–a large factory

rich–full of the food and water that plants need to grow

ton–2,000 pounds

Learn More

Books

Dobson, David. *Can We Save Them?*
Illustrated by James M. Needham.
Watertown, Mass.: Charlesbridge
Publishing, 1997.

Royston, Angela. *Recycling.* Austin, Tex.:
Raintree Steck-Vaughn, 1999.

Woods, Mae. *Protecting the Rain Forest.*
Edina, Minn.: Abdo Publishing
Company, 1999.

Web Sites

afandpa.org/kids_educators/index.html

planning.org/kidsandcommunity

Index

GR: I
Word Count: 231

From Rebecca Weber

I grew up in the country, so I have always loved nature. I enjoy teaching people about the world and how to take care of it.

DATE DUE

DE 14 '03			
JA 28 04			
SE 1 '04			
OC 19 05			
MY 4 '06			
OC 25 '06			
AP 20 '07			
DE 17 '08			
MR 16 '09			
MY 5 '09			
OC 15			
AP 10 '10			
JY 28 '10			
AP 25 '11			
OC 13 '15			
AP 2 1 '16			
GAYLORD			PRINTED IN U.S.A.